11 Delicious Romanian Recipes with Anecdotes

Haan Palcu-Chang
Artwork by Alexia Udriste

To Mama

Table of
Contents

Introduction

My grandmother and mother were born and raised in Transylvania, and my grandfather came from Oltenia. I grew up eating Transylvanian food because, as was quite normal in their generation, my grandma did all the cooking.

Romanian food is as in my soul as anything else I could imagine. I ate it almost every week, and have deep, nostalgic connections to the flavours and smells of a Romanian kitchen. But as a professional chef, I never thought to really cook Romanian food for clients; I focused primarily on the Asian side of my heritage when creating menus for the restaurants I cooked for. Perhaps I was never quite sure how eastern European peasant food would be received by a broader audience.

However, in February 2021, I was a chef at a Thai restaurant in Toronto that was, like almost every other restaurant in the city at the time, struggling to stay afloat amidst some of the most severe COVID lockdowns in North America. As cash flow became tighter and tighter, I decided to give up many of my shifts to keep my staff employed.

Thinking about what I wanted to do with my spare time, it dawned on me that I really wanted to share the Romanian food I grew up on with a broader audience. It was with this backdrop that Mamaliga Kitchen, my Romanian food pop-up, was born. We began doing takeout once every few weeks out the side door of the Thai restaurant (on our first day, we did ten orders). But as the weeks and months went by, and we started getting coverage from local and national news outlets, we began filling our once-a-month lunches with seventy to eighty guests at a time.

There was a real demand from the Romanian community in Toronto, which, though large, was deprived of any Romanian culinary scene outside of some delis and grocery stores. It's very hard to describe the feeling of seeing Mamaliga Kitchen grow as it did before my eyes. In truth, it was a very emotional experience.

As somebody of mixed Romanian ancestry with an inability to speak Romanian, I wasn't sure how the project would be received by "real" Romanians. However, the concept was completely and utterly embraced by the Romanian community and the smiles, laughter, and joy that we were able to fill our room with every few weeks was truly special.

So this little cookbook is an ode to some of the food we cooked at Mamaliga Kitchen and a short, personal snapshot into what Romanian food is to me.

Pofta buna

A note on authenticity

The notion of "authenticity" in food comes up a lot. I think what most people mean when they talk about an authentic recipe is that it's done like how they did it in the old country or how their mama or grandma made it. But I can tell you right now the recipes in this book will not be how your grandma made them.

For me, authenticity is about an individual's personal journey with food. How does a recipe you cook express your story? What insight into who you are is it giving the people you serve it to? I don't care much at all if your *pasta pomodoro* doesn't taste exactly like somebody's Italian grandmother's, so long as it is cooked with love and care, tastes delicious, and tells me a little something about you.

This booklet consists of very "traditional" Romanian recipes. However, I am a Canadian of Taiwanese and Romanian heritage who has cooked professionally in France, Denmark, Singapore, and Canada. My versions of traditional Romanian food are probably not going to look or taste like the Romanian food that your *bunica* made for you growing up. And you know what? That's really okay. These Romanian recipes are a reflection of my story, my palate, and my history. And in this sense, they are 100 percent authentic.

Chef's notes

I've written out all these recipes in grams and in "grandma measurements." It's the professional chef in me that has to have everything perfectly measured out to the gram. And if you'd like the recipes to turn out as perfectly as possible, I'd suggest you do too—digital scales are so cheap now they ought to be in every kitchen. But if you must skip the scales, by all means do. After all, your bunica certainly did not use them, I am sure.

For seasoning, I've stayed away from adding exact measurements of salt for everything. Seasoning is so subjective; it really is up to the chef. I've given precise salt measurements for sausages, meat fillings, and soup because many less-experienced home cooks might severely underestimate how much salt is needed to make these foods properly seasoned.

However, if a recipe looks like it has too much salt for your taste, add it in steps. You can always add salt, but you can't take it away. That being said, if the recipe tastes bland or just not quite right, it's probably because it needs more salt. Salt is not only salty; it is a flavour enhancer. The difference between a good restaurant-cooked meal and a bland home-cooked meal is often just more salt.

One last thing I will add is that though these recipes are humble in nature, they aren't necessarily meant to be easy or quick to prepare. There are probably less time-consuming ways to prepare all these recipes. However, I've settled on the methods I have because, for me, they result in the best possible finished product. Unfortunately, there are no shortcuts when it comes to delicious food. With this in mind, make sure to read the recipes all the way through before you start to cook them. Quite a few of them require long periods of soaking, resting, or cooking. So it's best to know what you are getting yourself into before diving into a recipe.

Salată de boeuf

Salad of poached chicken, root
vegetables, pickles, and mayonnaise

Salată de boeuf is a salad of boiled vegetables, meat, and mayonnaise that is often served on holidays in Romania.

For me, it's one of the most nostalgic foods I can think of, as it was almost always around at my grandma's house when I came to visit. Despite its name, my grandma only made it with chicken, not beef.

Though I'd found that odd as a child, I've since gathered that this is a pretty common variation on the classic recipe. And if I'm honest, having now tried the beef version multiple times, I still prefer the recipe with chicken. I find it's a bit lighter and easier to eat.

Of course, it goes without saying that my grandma's salată de boeuf was the best. But as I started developing my own recipe, I knew I needed to change a few things to adapt it to my own palate.

The problem with a lot of salată de boeufs is that they aren't particularly vibrant, balanced, or textural. On the contrary, they are generally composed of an ungodly amount of mayo, some extremely overcooked vegetables, and a few sad pieces of meat. If you're really lucky, you may get some canned green peas in there.

I imagine these versions of the salad being served at a low-level Romanian communist official's Christmas party in the 1980s. You get the picture—they're drab, cloying affairs.

I'm not saying this was my bunica's version, because she really did make an excellent one, but her insistence on using canned peas in her recipe did give it a flavour profile and texture that made it at least slightly Iron Curtain-y.

My recipe tries to be the opposite of that. The vegetables are blanched separately in batches until they are soft but have texture and structure. I've also upped the proportions of pickled vegetables, lowered the amount of mayo, and added lemon zest and juice for zing and vibrancy.

This method takes more time, but the end result is a salad that stays true to its roots yet has layers, depth, and balance. It's a surprisingly sophisticated eating experience for something that looks so humble.

Salată de boeuf

Ingredients

700 g bone-in chicken thighs

10 g or 2 tsp. salt

260 g or 3 medium-sized carrots, peeled and finely diced

150 g or 1 large parsnip, peeled and finely diced

150 g or about ⅓ large celeriac, peeled and finely diced

150 g or 1½ cups frozen peas

225 g or 1¾ cups dill pickles or gherkins, finely diced

100 g or ½ cup roasted peppers in vinegar, finely diced

125 g or ½ cup mayonnaise (I prefer Japanese Kewpie here)

1 lemon, juiced and zested

2–3 Tbsp. Dijon mustard

Kosher salt and pepper

Directions

1 Place the chicken thighs and salt in a pot, cover with cold water, and bring to a gentle simmer. Skim any scum that surfaces. Simmer on low heat until the chicken is cooked through and starting to fall off the bone, 25–30 minutes. Set the pot aside, and let the chicken cool to room temperature in the cooking liquid.

2 When the chicken thighs have cooled down, use your hands to shred the chicken meat off the bone. Roughly chop the chicken meat with a knife and set aside.

3 Return the chicken poaching liquid to the stove and bring to a boil. Add the carrots to the water and boil until fully cooked through but there's still a bit of bite. Remove the carrots with a slotted spoon and allow to cool to room temperature on a tray. Repeat this process with the parsnips, celeriac, and frozen peas. Add water to the pot if necessary to ensure that the vegetables can be blanched properly.

4 To finish, ensure the blanched vegetables are well drained and cooled to room temperature. In a large mixing bowl, add all the salad ingredients. Mix well and season with salt and pepper to taste. Serve immediately as a part of a meal or by itself with some good crusty bread

Salată de vinete

Charred eggplant salad

I can't be certain, but if I had to guess, I'd say that **salată de vinete** may be the most ubiquitous of Romanian dishes. It's eaten all over the country and is served as part of humble family meals and festive feasts alike.

It's a simple roasted eggplant salad, almost always eaten on or with a good piece of bread. And like all recipes with a very limited list of ingredients, it lives or dies on the love and technique you put into or add to it. Salată de vinete is nothing particularly inspiring to look at—it's just a bunch of mashed eggplant on a plate. But the best versions will have a depth of flavour that stands in surprising contrast to their ho-hum appearance. They will be smoky and well seasoned and have an almost unctuous mouthfeel.

For most people, their bunica's recipe probably involves grilling the eggplant on a barbecue or roasting it at high heat in the oven. But my family in Romania cooks their eggplant directly on cast iron, and that's how I do it too. The cast iron allows for a larger amount of the eggplant's skin to be kissed by intense heat, giving a level of char and corresponding smokiness to the eggplant that's hard to replicate with other methods.

After the eggplants are cooked, it's a matter of peeling them and letting them sit in a colander so they can excrete as much juice as possible. These cooking liquids can sometimes carry the bitterness that eggplant is often associated with, but more importantly, getting rid of as much liquid as possible will intensify the eggplant flavour. It'll be the difference between a watery, very "meh" vinete and one that is truly special. Don't skip this step. Like pretty much anything else in life, there just aren't any shortcuts that can be taken if you want to do this right.

Now, for the controversial part: when the eggplant is ready to get mixed in, I add a little mayo to mine. For the non-Romanians out there or those Romanians less encumbered by tradition, this may not seem like a big deal. But I know a lot of vinete purists are already hurling this recipe to the ground in disgust, so I feel compelled to defend my actions. I'm deeply sorry for the shame I've brought upon our culture. Truly, I am. But hear me out. First off, it's not a lot—a couple of tablespoons for 2 kg of eggplant.

Second, I often find that only using oil in your vinete can leave the final product tasting a bit astringent or a little harsh. A dollop of mayo rounds out the flavour and balances the dish nicely. I've served this recipe to literally hundreds of Romanians who would die on the "no mayo in vinete" hill, and not a single one has ever realized there was mayo in their eggplant. So, in the case of this recipe, at least, I think this is a mental hurdle to overcome more than it is a question of the eggplant tasting "bad." If you can't bring yourself to do it, don't. But you're missing out.

Salată de vinete

Ingredients

2 kg or 5–6 medium-sized eggplants

60 mL or ¼ cup olive oil

Kosher salt

20–30 g or 1–2 Tbsp. mayonnaise (I prefer homemade here if that is possible)

50 g or ¼–⅓ cup red onion, finely chopped

Directions

1 Heat a large cast-iron pan on high or medium–high heat. Make sure to turn your kitchen fan on high and open all your kitchen windows. This will get smoky. Place the eggplants in the pan with no oil. If not all the eggplants fit in the pan, cook them in batches. Cook each eggplant until deeply charred on one side. The surface will start blackening, and as the inside flesh cooks, the eggplant will start to flatten on the side you are cooking. When the first side is very charred, give the eggplant a quarter turn. Repeat until the entire eggplant is charred. The eggplant is done when a kitchen knife inserted into the middle meets no resistance.

2 Using a paring knife, immediately peel the cooked eggplant. Discard the skin and the top of the vegetable, and place the flesh into a nonreactive colander or strainer. When the flesh of all your eggplants is in the colander, allow it to drain for 3–4 hours. It's worth repeating: do not skip this step.

3 To finish, get a mixing bowl and mixing spoon. It's important that neither the bowl nor the spoon is metal. Metal reacts oddly with eggplant and can give it an unpleasant aftertaste. Put the eggplant into the bowl and beat well with the spoon. The eggplant should be so soft that it will start immediately breaking apart. This may take a few minutes, but it's worth the wait. The air you incorporate into the eggplant at this stage will help the finished product be lovely and light. At this stage, slowly drizzle in the oil while continuing to beat the eggplant. When the oil has been fully incorporated, add salt and season to your liking. Finally, mix in the mayonnaise. Serve immediately, with the onions on the side so people can add them to their salad as they wish. This dish is best eaten at room temperature on the day that it is made. However, it's still very good a day or two after if you have any leftovers.

Ciorbă de perișoare

Meatball soup

I'm not entirely sure there are a people who like soups more than Romanians. Growing up, when I would visit my grandmother's every weekend, there would always be a pot of soup warming on the stove. Chicken broth with noodles, rich vegetable soups with egg and flour dumplings, turkey soup with rice and speckled with parsley. A meal without *supica* was, well, simply not a meal. Consequently, I've carried a love of soup with me my entire life.

There's something immensely comforting about the simplicity of many Romanian soups. A few chopped vegetables. Some scraps of meat. Water. You have to dedicate time and care to these ingredients in order for them to meld together in a pot and become something delicious and nourishing. So when you are hunched over a bowl of a particularly tasty soup, you know it was prepared with a level of attention and care that can so often be missing from our modern, fast-paced lives.

The crown jewel in my grandmother's soup repertoire is **ciorbă de perișoare**, or, in English, meatball soup. And I suspect this soup holds a special place in the hearts of many Romanians. It's a festive, hearty dish full of flavour and good for any occasion. Ciorbă is a beloved subcategory of soup in Romania. It's a cousin to similar soups that are served all over other parts of eastern Europe as well as North Africa, the Near East, and Central Asia.

As a rule, ciorbăs have a distinctive, acidic tang. Usually, this comes from the addition of something called *borș*—a sour liquid made from fermented wheat bran and polenta. For those who want the real deal when cooking this recipe, we've included instructions to make your own borș. You'll need a little patience and a little planning, but the results won't disappoint.

However, for those who are more into immediate gratification and want their soup now, there's a shortcut that I am particularly fond of. Simply replace the borș with some naturally fermented pickle juice (no vinegar pickle, thank you very much). It's not traditional, but, to be honest, it does the trick quite nicely. And I find that on days when I don't think any Romanians are in earshot I almost prefer it to the original version. There's an added punchiness about pickle juice that satisfies my Asian sensibilities. There's no doubt that using pickle juice will give you a more in-your-face result. But it's delicious nonetheless and worth a try.

This recipe uses a lot of vegetables. But I've found this quantity brings a level of complexity to the broth that is hard to beat. I hate a watery, flavourless soup. And a high proportion of vegetables in a soup is a good way to avoid that. Plus, as a rule, I come from a family where soups were often stand-alone meals. We weren't much for sad, little bowls of broth with a few bits of meat and vegetables floating around. We were and are a hearty soup family, and that is reflected in most of my soup recipes.

Ciorbă de perișoare

Ingredients

For the borș (makes 2 L)

200 g or about 3 cups wheat bran

100 g or ¾ cup coarse polenta

2.5 L tepid water

15 g or 1 Tbsp. sugar

1 piece of very toasted toast

1 handful of parsley

2–3 bay leaves

2–3 sprigs of thyme

For the meatballs

250 g or scant ½ lbs. ground beef

250 g or scant ½ lbs. ground pork

1 egg

75 g or scant ½ cup rice, cooked in 75 g or scant ½ cup water until water is totally evaporated and cooled down (it will not be fully cooked)

8 g or 1¼ tsp. kosher salt

4 g or 1 heaped tsp. sweet Hungarian paprika

1 g or ¼ tsp. ground black pepper

A small handful of parsley, finely cut

For the soup

4–5 Tbsp. olive oil

125 g or 1 small onion, finely diced

125 g or about 1 medium carrot, peeled and grated

125 g or about 1½ small parsnips, peeled and grated

110 g grated or about ¼ large celeriac, peeled and grated

110 g or about ½ red bell pepper, finely diced

110 g or about 2 small tomatoes, finely diced

110 g or ½ large kohlrabi, peeled and diced (optional)

1 bay leaf

1 L chicken stock

1 L borș or 500 mL of juice from lacto-fermented cabbage or pickles mixed with 500 mL water

2 Tbsp. kosher salt (you may not need this if you are using pickle juice

To serve

An equal mix of lovage, flat parsley, and dill (a very generous handful's worth), finely chopped

1 Tbsp. sour cream per serving (optional)

Directions

1. **To make the borş,** combine 60 g of the wheat bran with 60 g of the polenta and mix with 200 mL of the water. Place the mixture into a sealed jar and leave somewhere warm for 12 hours.

2. Now open the jar and mix in the remaining borş ingredients. Cover the jar with the lid. Leave it somewhere warm to ferment for as much as a week. The quickness of the fermentation will depend largely on the ambient temperature. Stir the mixture every day with a wooden spoon. When it tastes sour and slightly sweet, it is ready to use. Strain the liquid through a fine sieve, and store it in a refrigerator until needed.

3. **To make the meatballs,** mix all the meatball ingredients vigorously in a bowl. The meat is properly mixed when you squeeze some in your hand and then open your hand with your palm facing down. The meat should stick to your hand. Now clean your hands. Dip them into a bowl of cold water and start making balls from the meat mixture. There's no "right" size here, but I prefer mine to be about half the size of a golf ball. Place the balls on a plate or tray, and keep them covered in the fridge until needed.

4. **For the soup,** set a large soup pot over medium heat. Add the oil and onions. Cook the onions until they are soft and translucent, 5–10 minutes. Next, add the carrots, parsnips, celeriac, and red pepper. Slowly cook these vegetables until they are soft and tender. Add the remaining vegetables and liquids to the pot and bring to a gentle simmer.

5. Carefully add the meatballs to the pot. If you are using borş, season the soup with salt. If you are using pickle juice, you may find that it is salty enough. Simmer the soup for 1½ hours until the meatballs are unctuous and tender. Do a final seasoning with salt, and if the soup seems to have reduced too much, add more water to achieve your desired consistency. Serve with the chopped herbs and a dollop of sour cream, if using.

Ciorbă de burtă

Tripe soup

Tripe is not an ingredient that people feel indifferent about. It can smell and taste a bit funky and has a very particular texture. You either like it or you don't. I happen to like it a lot. Funnily enough, my love of tripe didn't actually come from my Romanian side. My Romanian grandma was never very fond of offal. So tripe was out of the question, and we never had it in our house.

However, on my Taiwanese side, I ate it all the time growing up. It was in soups, rice porridge, steamed, and made into salads. And I've had a love for it ever since. In Romania, the most popular way to eat it is in ciorbă de burtă, or tripe soup. It's a much-beloved dish in many parts of the country, especially amongst the Transylvanian peasant stock that my family came from. And though recipes vary from region to region, the most common version of this soup involves some beef broth enriched with sour cream and egg yolk, seasoned with a bit of vinegar, and, of course, cooked tripe.

The acidity from the vinegar cuts through the tripe flavour, while the dairy and eggs give a really pleasing, velvety mouthfeel that makes the soup very easy to devour. The first time I ate this dish was when I visited Romania in high school. A cousin of mine was working at a 24-hour country restaurant that catered to shift workers and truckers. They were known for their ciorbă de burtă, and she took my family and me there with some of her friends.

When the soup was placed on the table, well, it looked pretty austere. It was a very plain, almost pathetic bowl of soup with a few bobbing bits of tripe in it. The cooks hadn't even given it the dignity of some sprinkled parsley on top. Of course, when I ate it, all my superficial judgment went out the window. It was bloody good. They served it with crusty bread and a fresh green hot pepper on the side. The combination of unctuous, creamy soup broth, velvety tripe, pungent garlic crisp bread, and the brightness and piquancy of a fresh chilli—just trust me. It's very, very delicious.

For me, the key to this soup is blanching the tripe three times in boiling water before you cook it. I like tripe. More than most. But even for me, unblanched tripe can just be too much. On the other hand, if you blanch it too much, it starts not tasting like tripe. And at that point, you have to ask yourself: "Why am I even cooking tripe soup?" Three times is my Goldilocks number. Do it more or less if you wish, but for me, this strikes the perfect balance between the main ingredient tasting like it's supposed to and not being too intense for your palate.

Chef's notes

This recipe is rather large, and it's because it's quite hard to buy just a little bit of tripe at the butcher shop. So you might as well make this for a party or freeze it and save it for later. Just make sure that if you choose the latter option, do not freeze it with the dairy or eggs added to the soup.

I'd also add that the level of garlic and vinegar in this soup works very well for my palate. But there's no denying that this recipe is very heavy-handed with both these ingredients. So, while these ratios very much work for me, I'd suggest allowing your guests to add the garlic and vinegar to their own portions of soup as they see fit.

Ciorbă de burtă

Ingredients

For the broth

2.25 kg or about 5 lbs. beef tripe (I prefer honeycomb tripe)

500 g or 1 lb. beef shin, sliced in 1-inch rounds by the butcher

70 g or ¼ cup + 2 tsp. kosher salt (add half to start and only add the remainder if you feel you need it)

225 g or 2 parsnips, peeled and cut into 2–3 large chunks

180 g or about ⅓ large celeriac, peeled and cut into 2–3 large chunks

525 g or about 4 small onions, peeled and cut into 2–3 large chunks

210 g or about 2 medium carrots, peeled and cut into 2–3 large chunks

2 bay leaves

¾ Tbsp. whole black pepper

For the carrot garnish

A few tablespoons olive oil

210 g or 2 medium carrots, peeled and shredded on a large box grater

A couple pinches of salt

To finish

9 egg yolks

750 g or about 1½ lbs. full-fat sour cream

To serve

75 g or 15 cloves garlic, minced very finely

175 g or about ¾ cup white vinegar

Directions

1   In a large pot, add the tripe and beef shin. Cover with cold water and bring to a boil. Immediately strain and rinse off any scum or impurities that have attached themselves to the meat. Repeat this process two more times.

2   Take the tripe and cut it into bite-sized pieces. Add the tripe, beef shin, and salt to the pot. Cover with cold water and bring to a gentle simmer. Simmer the tripe for 1½–2 hours, topping the pot with water throughout the cooking period so that the meat is always submerged. Test the tripe; it should be almost completely cooked but just a little too chewy. At this stage, add all the remaining broth ingredients. Once the soup has returned to a simmer, cook for a further 30–45 minutes until the vegetables are soft and the tripe is very tender. Remove from the heat and let cool to room temperature. This will allow the flavours of the broth to develop further and permeate the tripe.

3   In the meantime, make the carrot garnish. Heat the oil in a frying pan over medium-low heat. Add the carrots and a pinch or two of salt and slowly cook until the carrots are cooked through and very tender. Continually stir the carrots. If they stick to the bottom of the pan, add a small touch of water. It should take about 10 minutes for the carrots to cook. Place them aside when ready.

4   When the soup has cooled, fish out the vegetables and bay leaves. Discard them. You can also remove the black peppercorns, but I personally love biting into them—the spiciness cuts through the richness of the soup. Remove the beef shank and shred the meat off the bone with your hands, then add back to the soup. You can discard the shank bones.

5   To finish, bring the broth to a boil. While the soup is coming up to temperature, whisk the egg yolks and sour cream together in a bowl. When the soup is hot, take it off the heat. Take the egg mixture and slowly drizzle it into the soup, whisking vigorously the entire time. If you do not whisk with conviction, or you add too much of the egg mixture at one time, you risk splitting or curdling the soup.

6   Serve this soup immediately with the garlic and white vinegar on the side. Let each person add as much or as little garlic and vinegar to their portion as they desire. Let the soup stand for 3–4 minutes to lessen the intensity of the raw garlic. Taste for seasoning. Add salt or more vinegar to your taste. Garnish with a little bit of the grated carrot. You'd do yourself a great service if you ate this with some crusty bread and a raw green chilli on the side to nibble on between spoonfuls of soup.

Fasole bătută cu cârnați de casă

White bean puree with homemade sausage

This is one of my all-time favourite Romanian dishes. That may seem odd, given it's an incredibly simple dish—it's just a white bean puree served with caramelized onions and some fried sausage on the side. But I suppose being a humble dish doesn't mean it can't be special. And it's certainly special to me.

My grandma always used to greet me with a deep bowl, or Tupperware, filled with these beans when I came to visit. Hers were comforting, filling, and quite delicious. And I'd always fight with my grandpa over who got to smear their beans on their bread first.

Growing up, I spread the puree on my bread in a thin layer. It was very civilized and precise. But one year, during high school, I visited Romania with my mom and siblings, and I immediately realized I had been doing it all wrong. My uncle Liviu, whom we ate many meals with during that visit, had an incredible talent for heaping giant mounds of *fasole* onto his bread. It was wonderfully impressive from an engineering standpoint. And it was made even more so by the fact that he could not only stuff a massive piece of bread and beans into his mouth, but he could do so while simultaneously nibbling a bit of pickle and some cured meat, and managing to keep a toothpick dangling from the side of his mouth.

To this day, I am still left in awe of his oral dexterity. It was really quite inspiring. The point is, though, that I learned fasole is much more enjoyable to eat when you are jovially and industrially shoving it into your mouth. Any other way just won't do.

Traditionally, where my family is from, this dish is served topped with caramelized onions cooked in paprika and some fried or grilled sausages on the side. Both of which are very good companions to the creamy beans. My main gripe with many versions of this recipe is that they are stingy with the caramelized onions—you'll generally get just a few sprinkled on top—and when that happens, I always think to myself: "What the hell is the point?"

I like a lot of onions on my fasole, seasoned with a generous amount of sweet Hungarian paprika. I think the sweetness of the cooked-down onions and the very subtle spice of the paprika work well in cutting through the richness of the beans. So, in this recipe, there will be lots of onions.

Chef's notes

I've included a recipe for homemade Romanian sausages as well. Because that is traditional, and, well, my sausage recipe is pretty damn tasty. But, to be honest, growing up I ate fasole more often than not on its own with some bread and pickles. It really is great just by itself with some bread.

So don't let yourself get dissuaded from trying this recipe if you don't feel you have the time or skill to make sausage. That being said, if you do want to eat your beans with sausages but can't be fussed with sausage casings and sausage stuffers, make the sausage filling, form it into patties, and cook it as you would a hamburger. Or else you can grab a good garlic sausage (preferably with a bit of paprika in it) at the butcher or supermarket and make your life even easier. If you serve the fasole with sausage, it's common to serve it hot or warm. Without sausage, feel free to eat your beans at room temperature.

Fasole bătută cu cârnați de casă

Ingredients

For the cârnați (about six 130–150 g sausages)

1 kg or a little over 2 lbs. ground pork (with 30% fat)

20 g or 1 Tbsp. + 1 tsp. kosher salt

4 g or 1 tsp. ground pepper

35 g or about 7 cloves of garlic, minced

30 g or about 4 Tbsp. sweet Hungarian paprika

2–3 meters of hog casings, well rinsed

For the fasole

500 g or a generous 1 lb. dried white beans, soaked in cold water for 24 hours at room temperature and then drained well

180 g or 2–3 medium carrots, peeled and cut into 2–3 pieces

180 g or 1 large parsnip, peeled and cut into 2–3 pieces

300 g or about 2 small onions, peeled and sliced into quarters

200 g or about ¼ celeriac, peeled and cut into 2–3 pieces

5–6 sprigs of thyme

1 head of garlic, sliced in half horizontally

3–4 bay leaves

Kosher salt

For the onion garnish

4–6 Tbsp. vegetable oil

600 g or 5–6 small onions, finely sliced

4 tsp. Hungarian sweet paprika

Salt

Directions

1 **First, make the sausage.** Combine the pork, salt, pepper, garlic, and paprika in a large mixing bowl. Knead aggressively with your hands to properly emulsify all ingredients. To check if the filling is ready, grab a small handful and squeeze it. Now, open your hand with your palm facing down. The meat should stick to your hand. If it does, it means the proteins in the meat have been properly developed and will create a homogenous sausage.

2 If you do not want to case your sausage, you are done here. Portion the sausage into patties, and fry it up when you want to eat it.

3 If you would like to case your sausage, take the hog casings, tie a knot at one end of them, and prick a small hole with a toothpick right by the knot. Slide the other side of the casing onto a sausage stuffer, and fill the casing with the sausage meat until a large coil is formed. To create sausage links, use your fingers to make 5–6 pinches equally spaced along the length of the sausage. Twist the sausages several times where you made your pinches. Your sausages are now finished. Place them on a wire rack, and let them air-dry in your fridge for 24–48 hours. This step is not necessary but will make the sausages fry or grill up much crisper.

4 **To make the fasole,** place the beans, vegetables, and herbs into a pot and cover them with cold water. Do not put the salt in at this stage as it will harden the beans. Bring to a gentle simmer and cook the beans until very tender and just about falling apart, 1–2 hours, depending on the bean. Top the pot with water to ensure the vegetables and beans are always submerged. When ready, remove the beans from the heat and season with the salt. The liquid should taste very seasoned. Let the beans cool to room temperature in order to absorb all the seasoning and infuse the flavour from the vegetables and herbs.

5 Remove all the vegetables and herbs and discard them. Using a slotted spoon, transfer the beans into a food processor. Blend very thoroughly. You will likely need to add some of the cooking liquid to loosen up the mixture. When you have blended for at least 3–4 minutes, check for consistency and seasoning. For me, the perfect fasole resembles a slightly runny hummus. Set it aside until you are ready to eat. If you'd like to take an extra step to make sure your beans are very smooth, pass them through a fine-mesh strainer. But this step is not necessary.

6 **To make the onion garnish,** heat the oil in a pan over medium heat. Add the onions and cook with a few pinches of salt until they are soft, sweet, and starting to turn golden brown. Remove from the heat and stir in the paprika.

7 **To serve,** spoon the fasole onto a platter and pour all the onions over the top. Eat with the cooked sausages, a fat dill pickle, and some crusty bread.

Mici

Little Romanian sausages

Everybody loves grilled meat. Except those who don't. But those people usually aren't Romanian. If you visit Romania in the summer, I can guarantee you that there will not be a week that goes by without somebody inviting you over for a barbecue. It simply won't happen, at least not in the countryside where my family is from.

For Romanians, *mici* are the preeminent type of grilled meat at any barbecue. That may sound hyperbolic, but it really isn't. Ask any Romanian what they think of the combo of freshly grilled mici and cold beer. I don't think there's a duo out there besides Jesus and the Virgin Mary that elicits such heartfelt and religious reactions.

If you're from Bosnia and Herzegovina or Serbia, you're well acquainted with what mici *are*, because they are extremely similar to *ćevapi*. And in other parts of the Balkans, they'll have their slightly different versions too.

If you haven't had one, describing them doesn't really do them justice because they are truly a unique eating experience. In essence, though, they are uncased sausages that have had bone broth and baking soda whipped into them, which results in an incredibly juicy and slightly springy texture.

My first introduction to mici was through my grandparents' friend Unchiu Villi. He was always my favourite. My memory of him was a man full of life and love. I was particularly partial to him because, when he took my face in his two meaty hands and gave me the obligatory Romanian kiss on both my cheeks, he smelt good.

That is, he always applied the right amount of cologne. When he hugged me, the fumes emanating from him didn't singe my nostrils—something that couldn't be said for many of the other older Romanians I encountered throughout my childhood who always seemed to believe in a "more is more" philosophy when it came to eau de toilette.

Yes, Unchiu Villi was kind and warm, and I truly appreciated his perfumatory discretion. But really, if I am being honest, I loved him most because he would make his own mici at home and would very frequently bring them with him to the many Romanian gatherings I went to as a kid. Because mici were not readily available in stores when I was growing up, these were very special moments for me. I'd save my appetite until the first trays of mici came off the grill, then gobble them up after dipping them in some hot mustard. I wouldn't stop eating until I'd mostly become a mici myself.

Eat these freshly grilled with beer or serve them as part of a meal (also with beer). They go particularly well with roasted or fried potatoes and a simple cucumber salad with dill and white vinegar.

Chef's notes

The fat proportion in your meat is crucial for this recipe if you want to ensure the juiciest, most succulent sausages. Any good butcher should be able to get you ground beef and pork with the proper fat ratio. But if they don't, ground beef chuck and ground pork shoulder will get you approximately the level of fat you are looking for.

Most good butchers will also sell a high-quality beef broth. You are looking for the type of broth that will turn to jelly in the fridge. Or you can make it yourself by boiling roasted beef bones in water with a few aromatics for 4–5 hours.

This batch will make 25–30 sausages. They freeze exceptionally well in their raw form if you don't plan on eating them all in one sitting.

Lastly, and probably most importantly, the sausage mix should sit covered in the fridge for at least 12 hours before you portion and cook it in order for the baking soda to tenderize the meat and for the flavours to properly develop.

Mici

Ingredients

1600 g or about 3½ lbs. fatty ground beef (30% fat)

800 g or about 1¾ lbs. fatty ground pork (30% fat)

40 g or 2 Tbsp. + 1 tsp. kosher salt

6 g or 2 tsp. ground pepper

2 g or 1 tsp. dried thyme

6 g or 2 tsp. sweet Hungarian paprika

4 g or 1 tsp. ground allspice

40 g or 7-8 garlic cloves, minced

4 g or 1 tsp. ground coriander

12 g or 3 tsp. baking soda

500 g or 2 cups + 3 Tbsp. high-quality beef broth (it should turn to jelly when put into the fridge), just heated until liquid

Directions

1 Put all the ingredients except for the baking soda and beef broth into a stand mixer with the dough hook attachment on. Mix the ingredients on low and only until the seasoning has been evenly dispersed. Do not overmix. This should only take 1–2 minutes.

2 Meanwhile, in a small bowl, whisk the baking soda into the broth until completely dissolved. Slowly pour the broth into the mixer while the dough hook is still mixing. Continue adding the broth until fully incorporated into the meat, then turn off the mixer.

3 Make sure that the seasoning is evenly dispersed and there are no patches of unseasoned meat. If there are, gently mix the meat with your hands. At this stage, if you would like the best possible end product, you must put your sausage mix covered in the fridge for a minimum of 12 hours.

4 Portion into 80–100 g pieces and then shape into a cylinder that is 8–10 cm (3–4 inches). Grill or fry on medium-high heat until lightly charred on the outside and cooked through but slightly pink on the inside (the baking soda will keep the pork looking pink even though it is cooked through). If you have a digital thermometer, we find taking the sausages off at about 65°C (150°F) internal temperature and then letting them rest until the internal temperature reaches 70°C (158°F) before eating is the perfect formula.

Ardei umpluți

Stuffed sweet peppers

Stuffed peppers. Drool. These were a mainstay in my grandma's rotation. And it's not so hard to see why. They're incredibly delicious and can be whipped together without too much fuss. My grandma's version, on which this recipe is based, was made with red and yellow bell peppers, stuffed with rice, turkey or pork, and herbs, and simmered in a very light but flavourful broth.

I don't think you could say this is an inherently Romanian dish, as you'll find stuffed peppers in similar forms throughout the Balkans, eastern Europe, and the Caucasus. It seems like one of those dishes that probably sprung up simultaneously in many parts of the world, though I am sure there is a food historian somewhere out there ready to prove me wrong.

In Romania, they'd often use a local variant of the bell pepper that is a very lovely pale green or yellow. It's a bit longer and thinner than the ones you'd see in western European or North American markets. However, we didn't have those growing up in Toronto, so my grandma made do with the standard red and yellow bell peppers you could get at the local grocery store. So these are the ones we'll use for our recipe. They do the job quite nicely, and besides, I'm partial to the gentle sweetness they bring to the dish. It balances out the meatiness of the filling perfectly.

I'd just insist that you don't use dark green peppers for this recipe. There's no good reason for me to demand this of you other than I just don't like the taste of them in this dish. Consider yourself warned.

For the all-important stuffing, my grandma usually used turkey or pork. Over the years, I've personally gravitated to an equal mixture of pork and beef. The former gives the fattiness and juiciness, and the latter gives a hint of richness that elevates a simple dish into an eating experience that's a little more satiating.

We'd often eat these on their own with good, crusty bread on the side; there's too much good braising liquor in this recipe not to be sopped up with some lovely bread. However you decide to eat them, there is one nonnegotiable: when you've finished devouring your pepper, you must pick up your plate and slurp back the leftover juices.

Chef's notes

If you are using organic peppers, you may find that you need to double the amount of peppers for this recipe. Either way, it's quite possible that this entire recipe won't fit into one pot, especially if your kitchen is not equipped to feed a large family like mine is. So you can either halve the recipe or cook it in two separate pots if need be.

Ardei umpluți

Ingredients

A few splashes of olive oil

250 g or 1 medium onion, finely diced

A pinch of salt

145 g or scant 1 cup basmati rice

145 g or 1 cup chicken stock or water

For the filling

600 g or 1½ lbs. ground pork (20%–30% fat)

600 g or 1½ lbs. ground beef (20%–30% fat)

¾ bunch of dill, finely chopped

¾ bunch of flat-leaf parsley, finely chopped

2 g or ½ tsp. ground black pepper

16 g or 1 Tbsp. salt

8 g or 1 Tbsp. sweet Hungarian paprika

For the stuffed peppers

10 large bell peppers (red and yellow preferably)

750 g tomato puree (passata) + 8 g tomato paste mixed in

2 bay leaves

3–4 sprigs of thyme

Salt

Directions

1 Heat the oil in a pan over medium-low heat. Add the onions and a pinch of salt. Stir occasionally and continue to cook for 5–10 minutes until the onions are fully translucent and soft. When the onions are cooked through, add the rice and cook for 2–3 minutes until the grains have also gone slightly translucent. Add the stock and cook until the liquid is totally reduced. Set the rice on a plate in the fridge until fully cooled. The rice will not be completely cooked.

2 **To make the filling,** mix the ingredients with the cooled rice. Mix vigorously until the mixture is well combined. To check if the meat is at the proper consistency, squeeze a handful and then open your hand with your palm facing down. The meat should stick to your hand.

3 **To prepare the peppers,** cut the tops off with a knife. Remove and discard the stem. Set aside the pepper tops with the removed stems. Remove and discard the seeds from inside the peppers.

4 Stuff the peppers with the filling mixture. They should be filled until just under the lip of the top of the pepper. The rice will expand as it cooks, so it isn't ideal to have the peppers overstuffed.

5 In one or two large pots, equally distribute the tomato puree, tomato paste, herbs, and the tops of the peppers. Place the stuffed peppers on top of that mixture. They should be in one layer; do not stack them on top of each other.

6 Add just enough water to the peppers that it just covers them. Season this cooking liquid with salt to taste.

7 Cover the pot and simmer on medium-low or low heat for 1½–2 hours, or until the peppers are soft and tender but still hold together when taken out of the pot.

Sarmale cu mămăligă

Cabbage rolls with polenta

If there is one iconic Romanian dish, it has to be cabbage rolls with sour cream and polenta. When you think of many eastern European cuisines, you probably also think of cabbage rolls. But, and I say this with only the utmost journalistic integrity and objectivity, Romanian cabbage rolls are just better than those other versions. Full stop. Case closed. Very sorry.

I, of course, grew up eating my grandma's cabbage rolls. And they were always one of my absolute favourite things to eat. Mostly, they were for special occasions, but sometimes she would make them for me on a random school day when I came to visit, and those were always the best times. It felt like an early birthday or Christmas present.

My grandma would serve them hot, with a steaming heap of polenta and a dollop of sour cream on them. And I would definitely suggest this be the first way you eat these. But I won't lie: I've probably eaten them cold straight out of the fridge more than I have eaten them hot. I'm not sure if that style is for everybody, but it has worked for me, and some of my best food memories when I was younger involved sneaking into my grandma's fridge late at night to pop a few cold *sarmale* into my mouth before heading back to bed.

The thing you have to understand is that a good Romanian cabbage roll is a rather delicate and refined piece of craftsmanship. They're about the length of an index or middle finger (on a large hand like mine), and the filling of perfectly seasoned pork and rice should be wrapped in a thin but structurally sound encasement of naturally fermented sour cabbage leaves. The rolls should then be gently cooked in a beautifully flavoured broth enriched with smoked bacon, cabbage scraps, a few herbs, and a kiss of tomato until they melt in your mouth.

The finished product stands in stark contrast to the monstrosities you see in many eastern European delicatessens and restaurants in North America. You know the ones I am talking about—as big as a baby's arm, covered in bland tomato sauce, stuffed with God knows what flavourless filling, and (gasp) rolled in fresh, thick, unfermented cabbage. No. Just no. I'm feeling unsettled just thinking about it.

Chef's notes

The traditional accompaniment to this dish is *mămăligă*, or Romanian-style polenta. Polenta is often associated with the north of Italy, but it is probably the most favoured side dish in Romania, next to some bread. Though it seems such a simple dish, it actually took me weeks of trialling my recipe until I got the consistency and flavour that was right for me. The key here is using the high-quality medium-ground polenta you can get. It will make a huge difference. Fine polenta is, well, just too fine. And coarse polenta has a grittiness that I'm not particularly fond of. Once cooked, give it 20–30 minutes to rest off the heat to thicken up a bit.

If you are in an area without a large eastern European community and can't find sour cabbage, you'll have to make it yourself. For a quick pickle, take the leaves off a couple of regular-sized green cabbages. Place them in a large glass jar or food-safe plastic container. Fully submerge the cabbage in a salt and water brine. The ratio that works for me is about 3 Tbsp. or 45 g of kosher salt to 1 L of water. Once the cabbage is fully submerged, cover the container and let it sit at room temperature. It will take 5–10 days for the cabbage to develop a pleasing sour taste, depending on the ambient temperature.

Sarmale cu mămăligă

Ingredients

50 g or 2 Tbsp. + 1 tsp. vegetable oil

300 g or 2 small onions, peeled and finely minced

150 g or ¾ cup long-grain rice

150 g or ¾ cup water

Filling

1.5 kg or 3⅓ lbs. fatty ground pork

20 g or 1 large handful of dill, finely sliced (stems are okay)

20 g or 1 large handful of parsley, finely sliced (stems are okay)

10 g or 2 tsp. kosher salt

10 g or 2¼ tsp. chicken stock powder

1.5–2 kg whole pickled cabbage (amount will vary depending on the size of cabbages)

4–5 pickled cabbage leaves, finely sliced

650 g or 2½–3 cups tomato puree (passata)

250 g or generous ½ lb. country-style bacon, cut into 2–3 cm lengths and about 1 cm wide

4–5 sprigs of thyme

3–4 bay leaves

Directions

1 Heat the oil in a pan over medium heat, and add the onions. Sweat the onions until soft and translucent. Add the rice and cook for a few minutes until the grains have also started to become translucent. Add the water and gently simmer until it is fully absorbed. Set the rice aside and allow to fully cool. It will not be fully cooked.

2 Blend the rice mixture with the filling ingredients. Whip or beat the filling until well combined. When you grab some in your hand and then open your hand palm facing down, the filling should stick to your hand.

3 Now prepare the cabbage. Usually, the cabbage will have a hard stem down the centre. Cut that out with a paring knife. Roughly portion out 50 pieces of prepared cabbage for the rolls. The cabbage leaves will vary in size. You'll find that rolling the properly sized cabbage roll could involve anywhere between a half, a whole, or two leaves to adequately roll up the filling.

4 Prepare a heavy-bottomed pot to cook the cabbage rolls (the pot I use can fit 10–12 cabbage rolls in each layer). Sprinkle about a quarter of the sliced cabbage leaves on the bottom, and scatter a quarter each of the tomato puree, bacon, thyme, and bay leaves on top of the cabbage.

5 To roll the cabbage rolls, lay a piece of cabbage flat on a work surface. Put a heaping Tbsp. of the filling on the part of the cabbage that is closest to yourself. Now, make one roll upwards. Tuck in the two sides of the cabbage over the exposed tips of the roll, and then continue to roll upward. You should now have a lovely little cabbage roll with no filling exposed.

6 Place the prepared roll into the pot. Repeat until the bottom of the pot is completely covered in rolls. Now scatter another quarter of the cabbage, tomato puree, bacon, and herbs. Repeat this process until the whole pot is full and you have finished all the filling.

7 Just cover the cabbage rolls with cold water, cover with a lid, and bring to a gentle simmer. Cook at a very light bubble for 2–3 hours, or until the cabbage rolls can be cut with a fork or spoon and melt in your mouth. Check the cooking liquid for seasoning. Add salt if needed. You can eat these immediately, but I recommend you enjoy them the day after you make them to allow the flavours to mingle and develop. Serve with the mămăligă and a dollop of sour cream.

Mămăligă

Ingredients

900 g or about 3½ cups water

5 g or 1 tsp. kosher salt

180 g or about 1 generous cup high-quality medium-ground yellow cornmeal

A knob of butter

70 g or ¼ cup full-fat sour cream

Directions

1   In a pot, bring the water and salt to a gentle simmer. Gradually whisk in the polenta, making sure there are no clumps. Simmer at a very low temperature for 25–30 minutes until cooked. The mămăligă will splatter a lot and tend to stick to the bottom of the pan. Unfortunately, that's just the way it is with mămăligă! Because all cornmeal cooks differently, keep an eye on the consistency. It should resemble a wet porridge. If it is getting too stodgy or dry-looking, add more water.

2   When done, stir in the butter and sour cream. Let stand covered off the heat for a further 25–30 minutes to let it set and firm up. The finished product should not be runny. You should be able to spoon the polenta onto a plate without it running off the spoon.

Prăjitură cu mere

Romanian apple cake

If there is one food that stands out as my preeminent food memory, it's my grandmother's apple cake. For me, and probably all my siblings too, this was the holy grail of my grandma's cooking repertoire. It was the ultimate treat, and it always felt like the pinnacle of her expression of love to us.

When my grandma made this cake for us, she'd bake it in the morning, cover it in kitchen cloth, and place it on top of the fridge. I think it was her attempt at protecting it from our grandpa, who was notorious for sneaking in bites of this delicacy before any of his grandchildren showed up for a visit. I don't recall her ever being fully successful in her bid to keep her cakes unnibbled until we arrived at her place. But we appreciated the effort nonetheless.

Bunica's apple cake is my version of Proust's madeleine. Yes, it is a truly delicious recipe. But this cake is also more than that—it's moments in time, it's reference points, it's many happy childhood memories. I feel very lucky to have a recipe like this weave its way in and out of the entirety of my life. And I look forward to passing this recipe to you so that it can leave its rather delicious mark on your lives as well. There are a few versions of **prăjitură cu mere** you find around Romania. The most common one I've seen has two layers of doughy or spongy cake with stewed apples in between. These can be good, but they aren't the type I grew up eating. In fact, I haven't found an exact replica of my grandma's recipe anywhere on the internet. So I have to think she's contributed her own unique recipe to the pantheon of delicious apple desserts.

As an eating experience, it isn't so much a cake as it is a thin, rectangular pie. The flaky yet pliable dough is the perfect vehicle for delivering the apple filling to your mouth. This recipe makes a half restaurant-size sheet tray of apple cake. This might seem like a lot until you have your first bite. That's when you realize how you can't really ever have enough around. This is the type of dessert that everybody comes back six or seven times for in a sitting. It's the epitome of that timeless, comforting, and soul-nourishing combo of apple, sugar, cinnamon, and pastry.

Chef's notes

There is one eccentricity of this recipe. You must incorporate the butter into the dough with a food processor. If you do it by hand, you tend to need about double the sour cream in order for the dough to come together. The food processor disperses the moisture of the butter into the flour in a more even way. If you feel the dough is still too dry, even when using the food processor, add 1 Tbsp. of sour cream to the flour at a time until the dough comes together. That being said, I implore you to be patient. I have made this recipe dozens of times with these exact proportions; the dough will start off very dry-looking but will eventually come together.

Prăjitură cu mere

460 x 330 mm or 18 x 13-inch sheet tray

Ingredients

For the filling

3 kg or about 6½ lbs. apples (I prefer Honeycrisp), peeled and grated on a large box grater

100 g or scant ½ cup sugar

6 g or 2 tsp. ground cinnamon

Juice of 2 lemon (zest both lemons before juicing and reserve the zest for the dough)

For the dough

800 g or 5 cups flour

5 g or 1 tsp. salt

Zest of 2 lemons

400 g unsalted butter at room temperature, cut into large cubes

4 egg yolks

30 g or 2 Tbsp. white vinegar

120 g or ½ cup full-fat sour cream

To finish

1–2 eggs, well beaten

Sugar for sprinkling

Directions

1   Add all the ingredients for the filling in a heavy-bottomed nonreactive pot and cook slowly over medium heat, stirring occasionally, for 30–45 minutes. When the liquid from the apples has almost entirely evaporated, pour the apples onto a sheet tray and place them in the fridge to fully cool.

2   **To make the dough**, place the flour, salt, and lemon zest in a food processor and pulse once or twice. Add the butter and pulse until the mixture resembles sand. If you do not have a food processor, gently massage the butter into the flour between your fingers until a similar consistency is achieved.

3   Pour the flour mixture onto a countertop and create a well in the middle of the flour. Add the remaining dough ingredients. With a fork, whisk the wet ingredients together. When they are well combined, slowly start incorporating the flour mixture into the centre of the well. When the mixture starts coming together, and you can no longer use the fork, use your hands to gently press the dough together. Do not over-knead; stop working the dough as soon as all the flour has been incorporated. Set aside and cover with a cloth until the filling is fully cooled. You are not looking for a totally cohesive dough. It is okay for it to be a bit flaky or shaggy and not fully homogenous. As you roll the dough out, it will become smooth.

4   To assemble, divide the dough into two equally sized balls. Use a rolling pin to roll each ball into a rectangle that will fit into the baking tray. Your dough should be just under ½ cm (⅛ inch) thick. There will likely be excess dough that you will need to trim off.

5   Take one piece of dough and unroll it gently onto the bottom of the baking tray. This dough is forgiving. If it tears or you have not rolled out a perfect rectangle, use the excess dough to patch up spaces in the pan. Evenly distribute all the apple filling over the pastry. Now, lay the second piece of dough on top of the apple.

6   Heat the oven to 175°C (350°F), with the oven rack in the middle of the oven. With a pastry brush, brush the beaten eggs evenly over the top of the cake. Sprinkle a thin layer of sugar on top of the pastry. Bake the cake until the top is golden brown, 30–45 minutes. Let cool to room temperature before serving.

Papanași prajiti

Romanian doughnuts with sour cherry preserves and sour cream

Many countries have their version of a doughnut, and Romanians are no different. In Romania, you'll find two types of donuts that generally reign supreme: *gogosi* and *papanși*. Gogosi are hole-less doughnuts rolled in sugar and filled with some type of fruit preserve (plum jam is my favourite).

Gogosi are wonderful to eat, but they don't quite stir up the same type of emotions amongst Romanians as papanși. Start talking to a Romanian about papanși— especially one that lives abroad and has not been home in a while— and you will see what I mean. Their eyes will start widening, their mouths will start watering, and they'll begin waxing poetic about the qualities of this especially Romanian dessert to whoever is in earshot. And though I am unquestionably biased, it really isn't hard to see why papanși are so loved. They bring all the sweet, deep-fried goodness of a doughnut with an additional layer of eastern European homey decadence. What's better than sweet, fried dough? Answer: Sweet, fried dough slathered in sour cream and sour cherry preserves.

This is definitely one of those recipes that needs to be made in order to understand why it is so special. The addition of cheese to the doughnut batter creates an end product that's truly unique. When you bite into a papanși straight out of the fryer, it's at once crisp, chewy, moist, dense, light, and, in a way, slightly creamy.

Traditionally, you'd use sour cherry preserves to top your papanși. And this is one instance where I'd unequivocally tell you to stick with tradition. Yes, blackberry or blueberry jam could be serviceable alternatives in a pinch. But why? Sour cherries just work so brilliantly with this particular recipe; it's almost not worth your time using anything else. I'm being a bit dramatic, of course (blackberry or blueberry jam would definitely still be very delicious), but I think my point has been made. Try to source or make a high-quality sour cherry preserve before you attempt to make papanși (one that is syrupy and pourable as opposed to jellied). You won't regret it.

Chef's notes

In Romania, the type of sour cherry preserves we use for this dessert is called **dulceață de vișine.** The main difference is that the fruit is in a thick syrup as opposed to being in jelly form. If you can find or make dulceață, this really is the way to go. I've added my recipe below in case you're inclined to go the DIY route. That being said, you can use regular sour cherry jam if that is all you can find or all that you have the energy for. However, I'd suggest you warm it up slightly in a pot so it becomes a bit more pourable and easier to spoon over the papanași.

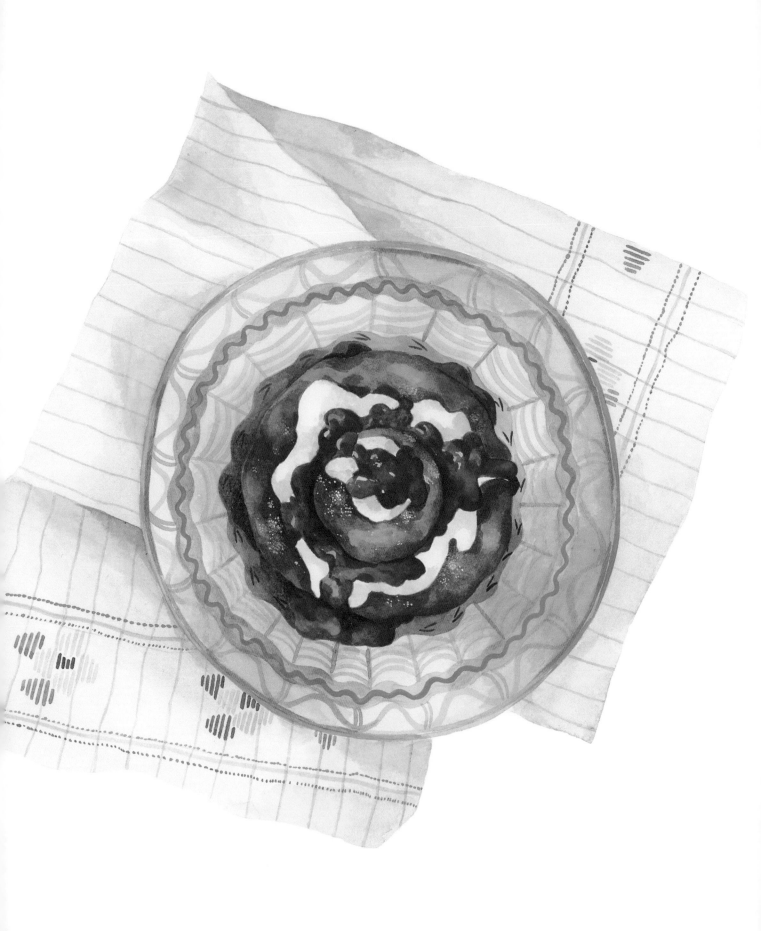

Papanași prajiti

Ingredients

For the doughnuts

500 g or 1 lb. + ¼ cup of ricotta cheese, left to drain in a kitchen towel or colander for 1–2 hours

2 eggs

5 g or 1 heaped tsp. baking soda

30 g or 2 Tbsp. sugar

5 g or 1 tsp. vanilla extract

Zest of 1 lemon

5 g or 1 tsp. kosher salt

5 g or 1 tsp. orange blossom water (optional)

250 g or about 2 cups + 2 Tbsp. all-purpose flour (more for dusting)

To fry

1–2 L neutral-flavoured cooking oil such as canola or grape-seed

To serve

200 g or scant 1 cup full-fat sour cream

150–200 g or scant 1 cup dulceata de visine or other high-quality sour cherry preserve

Directions

1 **To make the doughnuts,** mix all the ingredients except for the flour well until fully combined.

2 Gently mix in the flour a ladle at a time until fully incorporated and a slightly sticky dough is formed. Do not over-knead. The dough should be wet and sticky, but you should also be able to handle it without too much trouble. If the dough feels too wet to portion, add just enough flour to allow yourself to handle the dough.

3 Now, portion the dough into an equal amount of 120 g and 40 g dough balls. If you slightly wet your hand with water, it will make this process easier. If you have excess dough, either divide it amongst existing portions or make an extra smaller doughnut. Flatten the 120 g balls with the palm of your hand and poke a hole in the middle, gently enlarging the hole until you can fit the tip of two or three fingers inside. Leave the 40 g portions as balls.

4 Let the dough rest on the counter for 20–30 minutes, lightly covered with a kitchen towel.

5 In a heavy-bottomed pot or a deep fryer, heat the oil to 175°C (350°F).

6 Fry the papanași in batches, being careful not to overcrowd the pot. You can fry the 120 g and 40 g portions in any order you want. Cook for 3 minutes and then flip and cook for another 3 minutes. The 40 g balls could be hard to flip. If they are, gently keep them submerged under the oil with a slotted spoon until cooked. The papanași are ready when they are golden brown all over and a toothpick stuck into their centre comes out clean.

7 Let the papanași rest for 5–10 minutes. When ready to serve, place the larger portion of dough on a plate. Slather with sour cream and cherry preserves. Place the smaller dough ball on top of the larger doughnut's hole, and top again with sour cream and cherry preserves.

Dulceață de vișine

Sour cherry preserve

Ingredients

1.5 kg or 3⅓ lbs. pitted sour
cherries (frozen are perfectly fine)

1.5 kg or 3⅓ lbs. sugar

1 lemon, juiced

10 g or 2 tsp. vanilla extract

Directions

1 Place all the ingredients in a heavy-bottomed pot and gently simmer on medium or medium-low heat. It is important to skim off any scum that comes to the surface while cooking.

2 When the mixture has taken on a cough-syrup-like consistency, it is ready. This can take anywhere from 45 to 90 minutes depending on your stove and how much water is in the cherries you use. To make sure you have not over-reduced the syrup, place a spoonful of liquid on a plate and place it in the fridge for 10–15 minutes. If it completely hardens or is too hard to wipe off the plate with a finger, you will need to add some water to the pot to loosen up the mixture. You can store the dulceața in mason jars in the fridge indefinitely.

Albiniţa

Layered honey cake with Cream of Wheat
buttercream and raspberry jam

When people think of layered cakes, they'll often think of French patisseries. But let me tell you, Romanians know a thing or two about a good layered cake. So much so that I think it would have been impossible to include a section in desserts in this collection of recipes without including at least one layered cake.

Many of the cakes Romanians eat can be found in different parts of the world, but I've never seen anything exactly like albinița. Albinița means "little bee" in Romanian, and it gets its name from the honey cake layers that form the core of the dessert. This particular recipe is one of the few anomalies in this book in that there isn't really a direct connection to my grandmother. I don't think she ever made this for us, and if she did, I have no recollection of it.

Though my professional cooking journey into Romanian food was largely inspired by my grandma's cooking and food, like many Romanian grandmothers, she has a small, well-used repertoire of recipes that she returns to time and time again. And most of these are from the region she grew up in.

Trying to broaden my knowledge of Romanian recipes, I asked my mom if she had any suggestions. She told me about this cake somebody in her village made for her as a kid.

Albinița goes a little something like this: honey cake, Cream of Wheat buttercream, honey cake, jam, honey cake, Cream of Wheat buttercream, honey cake.

It is a bit of a pain in the butt to make, but when you bite into those sweet, beautiful layers, all the work really does seem worth it. Because I'd never eaten this cake before I made it myself, the recipe in this book is the culmination of hours of internet research and 10-12 trials before getting everything down to the point I was happy to serve it.

I'd highly recommend eating this with a good cup of Turkish coffee, as Romanians are wont to do, or, of course, an espresso will do in a pinch as well.

Chef's notes

An absolute nonnegotiable for this dessert to turn out properly is to ensure this cake sits at room temperature overnight before it is served. The honey cake essentially becomes a hard biscuit when it has cooled down. It's the sitting and pressing overnight that allows the Cream of Wheat and jam to soak into the dough and make it soft, unctuous, and ready for good eating.

Also, the thickness of the honey cake sheets is incredibly important. You must make sure that the dough does not exceed a ¼ cm (just over ¹⁄₁₆ inch) thickness. They will usually double in volume when baked, and if they are too thick, the layers will never fully soften. This recipe is designed to fit into a standard home baking tray. As all baking sheets are not the same size, use the thickness of the pastry as your main guide for determining the size of the cake.

Albiniţa

MAKES 15–20 TWO-BITE PORTIONS

Ingredients

Biscuit

150 g or ½ cup minus 1 Tbsp. honey

75 g or ⅓ cup butter

100 g or ½ cup sugar

550 g or 4⅓ cups flour

15 g baking soda

3 g or 1 scant tsp. kosher salt

45 g or 3 Tbsp. whole milk

1 egg

12 g or scant 1 Tbsp. vanilla extract

Cream of Wheat buttercream

300 g or 1¼ cups whole milk

75 g or ¼ cup + 1 Tbsp. sugar

5 g or 1 tsp. salt

80 g Cream of Wheat

5 g or 1 tsp. vanilla extract

200 g or ¾ cup + 2 Tbsp. butter at room temperature

350 g raspberry jam (the thicker, the better) with the zest of 1 lemon mixed in

Directions

1   **To make the biscuit,** heat the honey, butter, and sugar in a small pot until all the sugar has dissolved. Remove from the heat and let it cool until body temperature.

2   Mix the flour, baking soda, and salt in a large mixing bowl. Make a well in the centre of the flour. Add the milk, egg, and vanilla to the well. Now, pour the honey mixture into the well. Quickly beat the wet ingredients together with a fork.

3   Using the fork, slowly incorporate the flour into the wet ingredients. When it is too hard to mix the flour in with the fork, start using your hands to knead the dough. When the dough starts to come together and there are no longer any dry pieces of flour, it is ready. If it is still too dry and giving you difficulties, add 1 Tbsp. of milk at a time until a dough is formed. Do not over-knead.

4   Heat the oven to 175°C (350°F). Cut four pieces of parchment paper the size of the bottom of your baking tray. Now, divide the dough into four equal portions. Roll one portion out into as close to a rectangle as possible. Roll out to ¼ cm (just over ¹⁄₁₆ inch) thickness maximum. Add just enough flour to prevent the dough from sticking to the rolling surface. Transfer onto a piece of parchment paper. Transfer the parchment paper onto a baking sheet.

5   With a fork, prick the dough all over. It is important that the dough does not rise too much when baked. Bake for 10 minutes. The cake should just start to be turning golden brown and will be set all over. It should still be pliable but will harden significantly when cooled.

6   When the cake is done, transfer it to a cooling rack and repeat this same process with the remaining three pieces of dough.

7   **To make the Cream of Wheat buttercream,** heat the milk, sugar, and salt in a saucepan on medium heat. Bring to a gentle simmer, and then slowly whisk in the Cream of Wheat. Cook for a few minutes until the Cream of Wheat has thickened and is cooked through. Place a piece of plastic wrap directly onto the Cream of Wheat so that a skin is not formed. Let cool to room temperature.

8   Add the cooled Cream of Wheat to a stand mixer with a paddle attachment and begin mixing at low speed. Add the vanilla and then the butter spoon by spoon until fully incorporated. Once all the butter has been incorporated, the mixture should be light and creamy. Set aside.

9   To assemble, lay one layer of cake onto the baking sheet. Spread half the Cream of Wheat mixture evenly over the cake. Add another layer of cake on top of the Cream of Wheat. Now, spread all the jam and lemon mixture over this layer of cake. Top the jam with the third piece of cake, and cover this with the remaining Cream of Wheat. Flip the last layer of cake upside down, and place it on top of the final Cream of Wheat layer.

10 Wrap the baking tray very tightly with plastic wrap. Place another similar-sized baking tray on top, and put some weights on top of it (cans of beans or tomatoes work well here). Let sit at room temperature overnight at the very least, but preferably 24 hours before serving.

About the author

Haan is a chef of mixed Romanian-Taiwanese descent, born and raised in Toronto. He grew up eating sarmale at his bunica's and going out for dim sum with his Taiwanese family.

He has cooked in and led award-winning kitchens in Paris, Copenhagen, Singapore, Toronto, and Vancouver.

He currently lives on Salt Spring Island, British Columbia, with his beautiful little family.

About the illustrator

Alexia is a Romanian illustrator from Craiova. Her artwork is inspired by the Romanian countryside and by the plants and animals that live in the hills around her house.

When she's not painting, she's playing with her child and getting her hands dirty in her garden.

Printed in Great Britain
by Amazon

38381787R00037